You did not choose me, but I chose you and appointed you so that you might go and bear fruit – fruit that will last – and so that whatever you ask in my name the Father will give you.

John 15:16 (NIV)

Discipleship
in the
New Expedition

Phil Maynard

Discipleship in the New Expedition

books@marketsquarebooks.com
141 N. Martinwood Rd. Knoxville TN 37923

ISBN: 978-1-950899-54-8

Printed and Bound in the United States of America

Contributing Editor: Kay Kotan

This resource was commissioned as
one of many interconnected steps in the
journey of *The Greatest Expedition*.

GreatestExpedition.com

Table of Contents

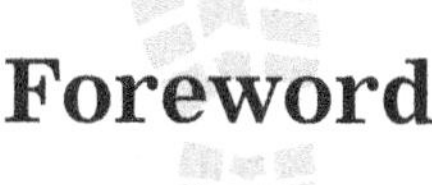

Foreword

This resource was commissioned as one of many interconnected steps in the journey of *The Greatest Expedition.* While each step is important individually, we intentionally built the multi-step Essentials Pack and the Expansion Pack to provide a richer and fuller experience with the greatest potential for transformation and introducing more people to a relationship with Jesus Christ. For more information, visit GreatestExpedition.org.

However, we also recognize you may be exploring this resource apart from *The Greatest Expedition.* You might find yourself on a personal journey, a small group journey, or perhaps a church leadership team journey. We are so glad you are on this journey!

As you take each step in your expedition, your Expedition Team will discover whether the ministry tools you will be exploring will be utilized only for the Expedition Team or if this expedition will be a congregational journey. Our hope and prayer is *The Greatest Expedition* is indeed a congregational journey, but if it proves to be a solo journey for just the Expedition Team, God will still do amazing things through your intentional exploration, discernment, and faithful next steps.

Regardless of how you came to discover *The Greatest Expedition,* it will pave the way to a new God-inspired expedition. Be brave and courageous on your journey through *The Greatest Expedition!*

Kay L Kotan, PCC

Director, *The Greatest Expedition*

INTRODUCTION
Discipleship

Discipleship is one of those topics that we talk about a lot in the church. Every church does discipleship in some form, yet most churches admit that this is an area with which they struggle to be effective and fruitful. Discipleship is not a new idea. It was certainly an expectation of Jesus who said in the Great Commission:

> *Go, therefore, and make disciples of all nations, baptizing them and teaching them to obey all I command.*
>
> **Matthew 28: 19-20 (NRSV)**

It is an expectation of the church today with mission statements like the following:

> *Make disciples of Jesus Christ for the transformation of the world.*
>
> **(Mission Statement of The United Methodist Church, *Book of Discipline***

But discipleship existed long before even the Great Commission of Jesus. There were disciples of Moses, disciples of the Pharisees, and even disciples of John the Baptist.

This, of course, raises all kinds of questions about what it means to be a disciple. In our modern context, we tend to describe disciples as "learners" or "pupils." This is true and is the literal meaning of the Greek word *mathetes.* What is less clear is the cultural context in which it is being used. Like many other words in use today, this understanding of disciple is far removed from the meaning of making disciples in the time of Jesus. Consider the following examples:[1]

THEN		NOW
Silly, foolish	Nice	Compliment
Worthy	Silly	Weak, foolish
Worth Awe	Awful	Terrible
Circle w/arms	Fathom	Understand
Ball of yarn	Clue	Evidence
Have nothing	Naughty	Behave badly
Young Knight	Bachelor	Unmarried man

(TED Talk, Anne Curzon)

1 Anne Curzan, Ted.com, *What Makes a Word Real?* https://www.ted.com/talks/anne_curzan_what_makes_a_word_real?language=en

The same kind of shift in meaning has occurred with the word "disciple." Consider the following:

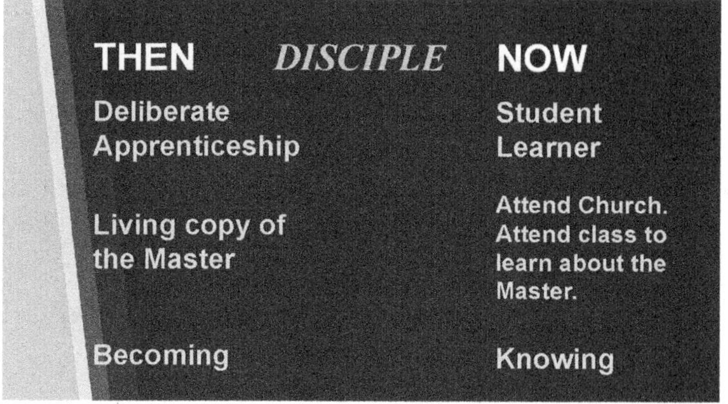

In our modern world, learners or pupils go to class in person or take online courses. That's how learning primarily takes place in our culture. In its original use, discipleship happened as one committed themselves to literally following the master (Rabbi, in the case of Jesus) and coming to know what they know and to do what they do. The goal of being a disciple was to become like the master.

Another nuance of the word disciple that has been lost in recent years is that the word disciple is both a noun and a verb. Note that the definition related to disciple as a verb is called "archaic" and "obsolete":

noun

Religion.

1. one of the 12 personal followers of Christ.
2. one of the 70 followers sent forth by Christ. Luke 10:1.
3. any other professed follower of Christ in His lifetime.
4. any follower of Christ.
5. *(initial capital letter)* a member of the Disciples of Christ.
6. a person who is a pupil or an adherent of the doctrines of another; follower: *a disciple of Freud.*

verb *(used with object),* **dis·ci·pled, dis·ci·pling.**
Archaic. to convert into a disciple.
Obsolete. to teach; train.[2]

The fact that disciple used as a verb is archaic and obsolete is a great loss for the church and illustrates just how far we have moved away from our Great Commission. This moving away from the Great Commission may indeed be a reason why your church needs an Expedition Team! We are called to be disciples (noun) and disciple (verb) others.

---

[2] Disciple, *dictionary.com.*

SECTION ONE

Themes of Discipleship

Jesus taught us how to disciple by example. Jesus commissioned us to make disciples by teaching/training them to obey. This is most fruitfully practiced as we issue the same invitation as Jesus: *come, follow me.*

That may take a variety of forms. For example:

- **Modeling:** a form of observational learning where the follower pays attention to exhibited behaviors and reproduces or copies that behavior.
- **Small Groups:** a limited number of disciples (Jesus had 12) who spend time together and learn from one another. John 3:22, for example, says Jesus "spent time" with his disciples. The Greek word for "spend time" is diatribe which literally means to "rub off on one another."

- **Teaching:** in the biblical sense this refers to direct instruction coupled with practical application. Bob Logan and Charles Ridley suggest the image of learning how to swim. Instruction is fine but there is no substitute for getting in the water and trying it. Mentoring: the process of guiding another person along a path that you have already traveled.

- **Apprenticing:** the transmission of specific skills from a person with expertise to a novice.

- **Coaching:** a partnership through which a disciple is able to discern what becoming like Jesus would look like in their context and develops a plan for moving toward that goal.

When Jesus gave the Great Commission to *wherever we go, make disciples of all the people groups,* he commissioned us to disciple (verb) people by teaching them to obey and baptizing them.

This is not an activity for a particular designated group, team, or committee. It is part of what it means to be a disciple. This happens at two or more levels. For example:

Level 1: Building relationships with people beyond the walls of the church, be the presence of Christ in their lives and invite them to discover the depths of God's love for them. This includes the opportunity for that person to make an initial commitment to become a disciple of Jesus.

Level 2: Supporting the development of growth in a disciple of Jesus as they commit themselves to become more like Jesus. This may include mentoring, apprenticing, modeling, teaching, and coaching. The focus at this level is the growth toward maturity of the disciple.

In all forms there are some themes that emerge related to an effective and fruitful pathway for discipleship. Discipleship is: relational, focused, intentional, developmental, and accountable. Let's take a look at each of these key areas of a pathway for discipleship.

Relational

Discipleship happens in relationships. It's a "contact sport." When we want to help someone grow as a disciple, our first impulse should not be to give them a book or training guide (although these may be helpful resources) and send them off to a corner to process what they're reading. We invite them into a relationship with someone further along the path of discipleship.

This discipler (partner) walks alongside the disciple. When the junior partner doesn't understand something, the discipler explains it. When they stumble, we help them up and dust them off. When they start off on a "rabbit trail," we bring them back to focus. When they need a helping hand, we reach out. When they experience success, we celebrate with them and for them!

Consider these words of the Apostle Paul:

> *For you know that we dealt with each of you as a father deals with his own children, encouraging, comforting and urging you to live lives worthy of God, who calls you into his Kingdom and glory.*
>
> **1 Thessalonians 2:11-12, (NIV)**

Discipleship is relational.

Focused

If we are to proceed according to Stephen Covey's call to "begin with the end in mind," before we can partner with someone to help them get somewhere, we must be clear about our destination.

Good disciplers help people see the end-goal of the process (becoming more like Jesus). They help the disciple keep their eyes on the target. In Matthew 14, Peter gets out of the boat and walks on the water toward Jesus. Everything goes great until he gets distracted by the wind and waves. When he takes his eyes off Jesus, he begins to sink. In the same way, the disciple must keep their eyes on Jesus. A disciple must stay focused to become more like Jesus.

Intentional

If we are in pursuit of a clear goal, it just makes sense to do specific things that will support movement toward that goal. This is intentional discipleship. It may be a great thing to have disciples engage in the newest "talking head" video study of the Bible (with lots of available choices for your favorite popular preacher/teacher of the moment). But, if the goal is to encourage a specific waypoint – say, a life of generosity, as an example – perhaps the training should be intentionally focused on biblical financial management. If the goal is developing a growing awareness of the presence of God, perhaps the training should introduce the breadth of spiritual practices that help develop this awareness. You get the idea. This is not to say that we shouldn't use "talking head" video series, just that we should be intentional about how we guide people toward their goals of maturing as a disciple.

Developmental

Discipleship is about growth. It's about movement toward something (an important distinction since, after all, even "backsliding" is a form of movement). In the previous section, we presented this growth as a continuum of behaviors that reflect a trajectory of development. This developmental aspect is not limited to behaviors which are considered official "spiritual practices." We cannot separate our spiritual lives from our physical lives or our emotional lives. As Jesus reminded us in the Great Commandment, which he said summarizes all the teachings and the law:

> *Love the Lord your God with all of your heart, soul, mind, and strength.*
>
> **Matthew 22:37**

Good discipleship is holistic. It is about developing our entire being.

Accountable

Effective discipleship includes an element of accountability. Jesus didn't just tell them how Kingdom life was done, or even just demonstrate how Kingdom life was done. He held the 12 accountable for developing a Kingdom perspective and practices. However, remembering that we are not Jesus, this role of holding folks accountable has practical limitations. The discipler is not the disciple's mother, supervisor, or boss. The discipler is the disciple's partner. The disciple is not accountable to the discipler as an individual. They are ultimately accountable to God and to themselves.

To the extent that we enter into accountability partnerships with anyone (discipler, disciple, mentor, coach, or small group partners), it is a voluntary, free will, non-compulsory relationship. It is fed by honesty, trust, compassion, and love. We may ask an accountability partner how something is working, what they are learning, where they are in the process, all of which are ways of providing accountability. But they are accountable to God and themselves. We are not issuing grades. We are not giving final exams.

Poorly executed accountability arrangements have destroyed many discipling relationships. Accountability is important, but it must be structured wholesomely and humbly. Expectations are important because people aspire to live into expectations. Expectations, however, must always be anchored in love because love is not a shackle. Love is a bridge.

SECTION TWO

What Discipleship Looks Like

If we as the Expedition Team are on a journey to make disciples, it would be important for us to be able to identify a disciple. There are a lot of opinions about what maturing disciples do, the perspectives they have, and the attitudes they exhibit as a way of being. In his book *Maximum Faith, George Barna* identifies 28 behaviors drawn from the scriptures. Covenant Discipleship, modeled after the work of John Wesley, the founder of the Methodist movement, identified nine key practices/behaviors for which class members were accountable for developing.[3]

It is important to note that in contrast to the perspective of many congregations, discipleship is about how we *live* rather than what we *know*.

---

3 See https://www.umc.org/en/content/covenant-discipleship-changing-lives-transforming-communities for more information on Covenant Discipleship.

> *Discipleship is not just about information. It is about transformation.*
>
> *Discipleship is not just about knowledge. It is about behaviors.*

There is no multiple-choice final exam. There is the affirmation *"well done good and faithful servant."*

As the missionary and founder of the Missional Church Movement, Alan Hirsch writes:

> *I simply do not believe that we can continue to try to think our way into a new way of acting, but rather, we need to act our way into a new way of thinking...*[4]

Or, consider the words of Dallas Willard, professor and leading thinker, about discipleship:

> *...the transformation of character comes through learning how to act in concert with Jesus Christ. Character is formed through action, and it is transformed through action, including carefully planned and grace-sustained disciplines...*[5]

---

4 Alan Hirsch,The Forgotten Ways, Brazos Press, 2006, pp.133-134.

5 Dallas Willard, *The Spirit of the Disciplines,* HarperCollins Publishing, p.158.

Based on our study of dozens of systems of discipleship and our interaction with a wide range of congregations utilizing these systems in real-world applications, we have summarized these behaviors with the following definition:

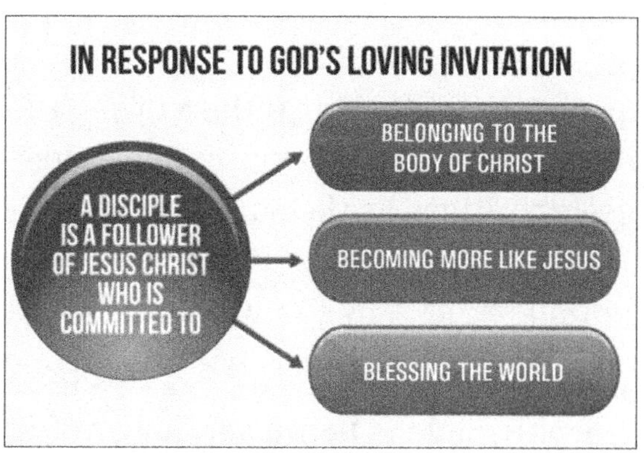

For those seeking a "biblical" basis for this definition, look no further than Matthew 4:19, where Jesus offers this quixotic invitation:

"Come, follow me" =
Belonging to the Body of Christ.

"And I will make you" =
Becoming more like Jesus.

"Fishers of men" =
Blessing the world.

These are three broad categories of behaviors (or ways of being). Jesus doesn't get into the nitty-gritty details of the "what" or "how" within these categories, and that's intentional. That comes later. This Matthew 4:19 invitation – which, after all, marks the very beginning of the apostles' mind-boggling journey – sketches the basic outline of the three major pillars of the life of an authentic disciple. Picturing these three discipleship pillars as the supports of a three-legged stool might be helpful. Each leg is equally important. The foundation is sturdy and stable only if each leg is equally strong.

Being a disciple is being a follower of Jesus Christ *for life*. Retirement is not the end goal of the discipleship career path. We keep on keeping on, always honing our discipleship skills, behaviors, traits, and practices. This is possible because of the creative flexibility incorporated within the discipleship process as modeled by Jesus. There is no one rigid accreditation standard: do these ten things in exactly this way, and you get your discipleship merit badge! We are free to explore our individualized path to discipleship. For each of the three categories represented in the three-legged stool illustration (each of three separate but interrelated ways of being), there are many different routes one can take to fulfill one's unique future within that category (belonging to the body of Christ, becoming more like Jesus, and blessing the world).

In the category of ***belonging to the body of Christ***, disciples discover deep relational connections with God and with one another. These relationships foster support, encouragement, challenge, accountability, and inspiration. Ultimately, we answer our call to grow the body by connecting with all the people beyond the walls of the church, as we are equipped to invite others to discover God's love for themselves.

In the category of ***becoming more like Jesus,*** disciples engage in the spiritual practices modeled by the Messiah that keep us in connection to God's grace, help form our lives to the will of God, and provide opportunities for us to help others grow in their discipleship.

In ***blessing*** **the world**, disciples discover the joy of giving of themselves and their resources to meet the needs of others. They use their gifts, talents, time, and financial resources to serve and make a Kingdom difference, addressing both mercy and justice issues, just as Jesus did.

We will focus together on a menu of specific behaviors and practices that can help us live into these unique ways of being. However, the goal of discipleship is not just to check these practices off a to-do list but to allow them to transform us into new ways of thinking and living. Changed behaviors lead to transformed lives. But the goal is not the accomplishment of the changes themselves. George Barna makes this distinction clear:

> *[T]he term transformation is not synonymous with the word change. The two terms differ in scope and significance. . . . Change is a refinement that is typically short-term, impermanent, incremental, superficial, and of limited ultimate consequence. In contrast, transformation is generally long-term, permanent, systemic, deep, and monumental in its impact and consequences. Change merely alters a known reality; transformation radically redefines that reality. . . . God wants you to be transformed.* [6]

What belonging to the body of Christ, becoming more like Jesus, and blessing the world will look like in the life of any individual

---

6 George Barna, *Maximum Faith,* Metaformation, 2011, pp.6-7.

disciple will overlap with what those ways of being look like for other disciples, but it may also be distinctly different. There is no set curriculum or cookie-cutter approach. There is no one-size-fits-all box into which we are required to squeeze.

For example, one disciple may find that the spiritual practice of contemplation is the most helpful way for them to experience that deep connection with God and God's grace. Another may find that an intensive study of Scripture is the most helpful. Both will engage the Word, but in ways that meet God's unique calling on their lives. Phil worked with a wonderful disciple who found God speaking in his life through intensive study of the Scriptures (what they call *exegesis* in seminary). This kind of study profoundly affected this disciple's view of the world. However, as studious as he was, he could never wrap his head around Phil's love for the technique of using guided meditations to reflect on select Scripture passages. They both found the Word to be a source of inspiration and guidance. God just wired them with different ways to get there.

One disciple may find a calling to serve the working poor in their neighborhood, while another may be called to go to Africa and provide wells for communities in need of clean water. Both are discovering the joy of giving of themselves and their resources to meet the needs of others. A guy we know named Joe has had a successful career in developing and running a coaching business serving non-profit service organizations around the southeastern U.S. He has been blessed with amazing success. He recently started volunteering as a mentor for local high school students. Not long ago, he said, "I feel like this is God's new calling for my life. It is such a blessing to help these young people see possibilities for their lives." On the other hand, Sarah just returned from a trip to Mozambique, where she provided prayer support for a mission team on site. Both have discovered the joy of giving themselves to others. Both ways are valid and honor God.

Despite their differences in application, these examples demonstrate how committed disciples move from concepts to action. We internalize what we learn, then work out our unique calling to put principles into practice.

SECTION THREE

Governance and Mobilization

To get us closer to the practical behaviors which are expressed within each of the ways of being a disciple (belonging to the body of Christ, becoming more like Jesus, and blessing the world), we have found it helpful to break out some "lifestyle" categories within each dimension of discipleship. We will take a deeper dive into each of these six lifestyle categories.

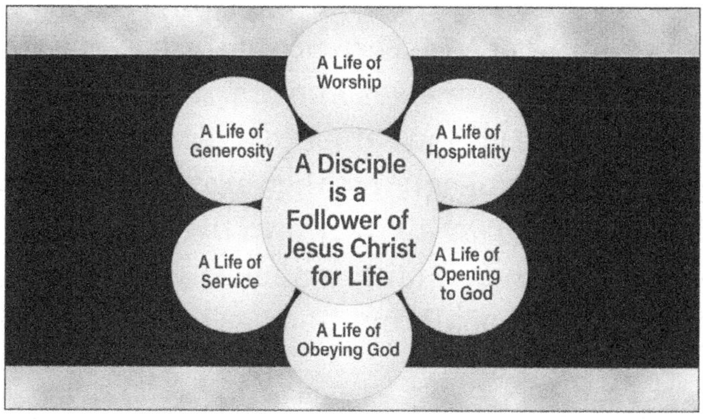

Belonging to the Body of Christ through a Life of Worship

Disciples are designed to worship God. As songwriter Louis Giglio puts it:

> *You are and always will be a worshiper.*
> *It's what you do.*
> *You can't help it.*
> *You can't stop.*
> *You can't live without it.*
> *But you can choose where you invest it.*
> *We're created to worship.*[7]

Notice the language. This includes participating in worship together, an activity that has been a focus of the people of God for thousands of years and through which we are drawn into a deep experience of the presence of God and offer ourselves into that relationship. As the people of God gather to offer a chorus of praise and thanksgiving, they are witnesses to the amazing grace in their own lives and the life of their chosen faith community. They join in celebration of all that God has been and will

---

7 Louis Giglio, "The Air I Breathe", *Wired for a Life of Worship*, Multnomah Books, 2006.

be doing in their midst. But a life of worship is bigger than attendance at corporate worship. It is about a daily lifestyle in which we are drawn into God's presence through our personal devotions. It's about cultivating an awareness of God's presence in the way all of life is lived. We see this in the stories of faith heroes like Brother Lawrence, as recounted in *The Practice of the Presence of God*:

> *We find him worshiping more in his kitchen than in his cathedral; he could pray, with another:*
>
> > *Lord of all pots and pans and things . . .*
> >
> > *Make me a saint by getting meals*
> >
> > *And washing up the plates!*
>
> *And he could say, "The time of business does not with me differ from the time of prayer, and in the noise and clatter of my kitchen, while several persons are at the same time calling for different things, I possess God in as great tranquility as if I were upon my knees at the blessed sacrament."*[8]

A life of worship means we make our relationship with God a priority by spending

---

[8] Brother Lawrence, *The Practice of the Presence of God*, Spire Books, 1958.

time devoted to building that relationship through praise, prayer, meditation, and reflection on the Scriptures and life. But it also includes honoring God in the ways we live our daily lives. To worship is to bring honor and glory to God. This includes a breadth of opportunities, including how we choose to use the resources God has provided to us, how we care for creation, how we engage other people and see them in the image of God, and how we do our jobs., We are offering our best as though serving God directly rather than just earning a paycheck.

Jesus modeled a life of worship:

- **John 4:23-24** (when he prophesies that a time is coming in which "true worshipers will worship the Father in spirit and in truth").
- **Matthew 4:10** (when he chastises the devil with the rejoinder that one should "worship only God").
- **Matthew 26:26-27** (when he leads the disciples in the Last Supper by instructing them, "Take and eat; this is my body" and "drink [from this cup]").

But his worship life was not merely centered around organized gatherings with readily recognizable aspects of what we would consider formal worship. Everything about his life was designed to bring honor and glory to God, from his disdain for materialism and the trappings of fame and power, to his teaching, to his miracles, to his concern for society's outcasts:

- He welcomed the refugees and the rejects with the hospitality of God.
- He went off by himself to spend time alone with God.
- He went to the temple and gathered his disciples in times of the religious feasts in Jerusalem.
- He celebrated the offerings of tears and expensive perfumes, as well as the widow's mite.

We, too, are called to his model of offering our lives in worship in these ways.

Belonging to the Body of Christ through a Life of Hospitality

Disciples have experienced the amazing hospitality of God first-hand. Through the grace of Jesus Christ, we have been loved, accepted, and welcomed into the Body of Christ. We, in turn, are called to offer that same hospitality to this world that God has loved so much that God gave his Son that it might be redeemed. Hospitality is an expression of God's love through us. This is bigger than shaking a hand or offering a seat in worship. Hospitality is making room in our lives for "the other." It doesn't matter whether "the other" is a fellow member of the Body of Christ, a neighbor, a stranger from the community, or a traveler from a distant land. The other person doesn't have to be like us or meet some artificial standard we have set. They don't have to be from the same ethnic, racial, socio-economic, or lifestyle group as us. Henri Nouwen, Roman Catholic priest, and author, puts it this way when he describes the ministry of presence:

> *It is a privilege to have the time to practice this simple ministry of presence. Still, it is not as simple as it seems. . . . I wonder more and more if the first thing shouldn't be to know people by name, to eat and drink with them, to listen to their stories and tell your own, and to let them know . . . that you do not simply like them – but truly love them.*[9]

Jesus modeled a life of hospitality. No one was outside the circle of his loving acceptance

---

9 Henri Nouwen, as quoted by Eric Cooter, *Ministry Matters*, 2013.

and care. He welcomed tax collectors, sinners, the woman at the well, and the woman who had been caught in the act of adultery. He calls us to follow his lead with compassion and empathy:

- He calls us to invite the poor, crippled, lame, and the blind (Luke 14:13).
- He calls us to show hospitality to strangers (Matthew 25:35).
- He calls us to give a cup of cold water to the thirsty (Mark 9:41).
- He calls us to welcome the children (Luke 18:15-17).

We, too, are to look for opportunities to extend God's gracious welcome to all.

Becoming More Like Jesus through a Life Opening to God

Any relationship is grown and enhanced as we spend time together and focus on one another. Disciples recognize that their relationship with God follows the same pattern. Disciples engage in spiritual practices that provide an ever-deepening connection to God and place themselves in the flow of God's grace into their lives. That grace is a free, unmerited gift of God's love, and disciples seek to be open to that flow of grace as they make that relationship a priority.

We use the following image to help describe this process of engagement:

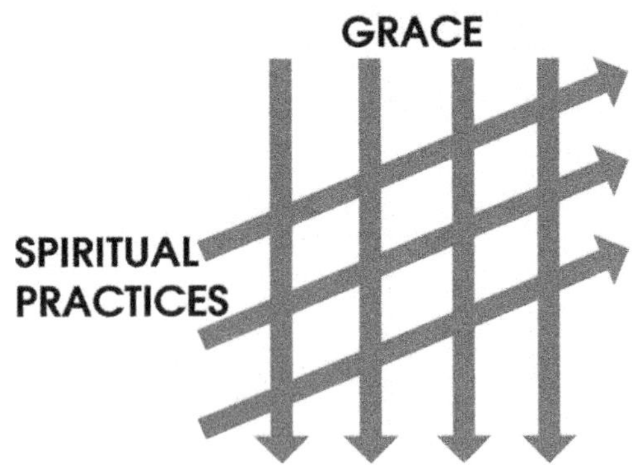

Jesus modeled this life opening to God as he:

- Engaged in solitude
- Prayed
- Encouraged fasting
- Quoted Scripture
- Worshiped

We, as disciples, are called to the spiritual practices that open us to God's love and grace through Jesus Christ.

Becoming More Like Jesus through a Life Obeying God

The Scriptures tell us that to Jesus, "all authority has been given . . . on heaven and on earth" (Matthew 28:18). Disciples of Jesus discover that obeying God brings abundant life. When we do what he tells us to do, our lives are lived in the will of God, just as Jesus the Son's life was lived in the will of God the Father. This dimension of obedience builds on the life opening to God as a disciple moves from the experience of God's grace in their own life to the sharing of God's grace with others through changing their behaviors to align with God's teaching. The more a disciple discovers of God's truth, the more change results. As a disciple embraces this Jesus-oriented life, they discover that they are transformed and thus become agents of transformation in the wider world.

Jesus modeled this life of obedience to God:

- drawing on Scripture to make decisions (for example, in his confrontation with Satan)
- welcoming the sinner
- discipling others
- seeking God/God's will through prayer
- giving his life on the cross.

Eugene Peterson describes the way this attitude of obedience takes shape within us:

> *[W]e are formed by the Holy Spirit in accordance with the text of Holy Scriptures. God does not put us in charge of forming our personal spiritualities. We grow in accordance with the revealed Word implanted in us by the Spirit.*[10]

Disciples of Jesus do the things Jesus says to do. They replicate the attitudes and actions that Jesus modeled. They even become disciplers of others in his name (people who intentionally guide other people in the process of discipleship).

Blessing the World through a Life of Service

Disciples live out the joy of serving others. They find that blessing others through their words and deeds brings a sense of blessing to their own lives. Just as Jesus modeled a life of service, his followers support the needy by feeding the hungry, healing the sick, clothing the naked, ministering to those who are prisoners (both the incarcerated and those imprisoned by their own economic circumstances, toxic relationships, and mental issues) – which we call mercy ministries. They

---

10 Eugene Peterson, Eat This Book, Eerdman's Publishing, 2006

also engage the powers of society to seek justice for the oppressed, outcast, impaired, and those unable to fend for themselves – which we call social justice ministries.

Jesus modeled a life of service every time he:

- Healed the sick (Matthew 8:1-3, in which he healed a leper)
- Fed the hungry (Matthew 14:13-21, in which he fed the 5,000)
- Attacked the systems that abused the poor. (John 2:13-22, in which he cleared the temple courts.)

Disciples of Jesus, likewise, develop a lifestyle of serving others. John Wesley, theologian and founder of the Methodist Movement, puts it this way:

Do all the good you can.

By all the means you can.

In all the ways you can.

In all the places you can.

At all the times you can.

To all the people you can.

As long as ever you can.[11]

---

11 See www.passiton.com/inspirational-quotes/7155-do-all-the-good-you-can-by-all-the-means-you.

Blessing the World through a Life of Generosity

Disciples of Jesus discover the blessings of using their resources, time, energy, and skills to have an impact in the world. They live within financial margins (spending less than they earn) so that they can respond to needs that God puts in their path. They support the Kingdom work by their tithes and offerings so that the church might have the resources to transform the world. Disciples recognize that everything they have and all the resources with which they have been blessed are gifts from God, who trusts them to use those resources wisely. We don't own them. God does. They are merely "on loan" to us, as stewards, to be managed faithfully, ethically, and responsibly.

Jesus modeled a life of generosity:

- He pointed to the sacrifice of the widow's mite. (Luke 21:1-4)
- He called us to give to God what is God's. (Mark 12:17)
- He willingly gave up his own life on the cross for our redemption. (John 15:13 and John 3:16)

Disciples of Jesus develop a lifestyle of generosity. Again, John Wesley, in a sermon called "The Use of Money," has coined a pithy set of phrases that boil the principles of godly generosity down to their essentials:

- Earn all you can.
- Save all you can.
- Give all you can.[12]

While we have identified some behaviors modeled by Jesus, as well as important principles that Jesus taught, the goal is not just to simulate those behaviors or parrot those teachings like some apostolic automaton. The goal is to have those behaviors and principles become so ingrained in our decision-making process that our whole way of living moves closer to God's holy standards. In theological terms, we call this process *sanctification*. The Holy Spirit works in and through us so that we may become more Jesus-like in every aspect of who we are and what we do.

Religious thinkers for two millennia have suggested ways to describe this process of

---

[12] See www.resourcesumc.org/en/content/john-wesley-on-giving.

ongoing transformation. John Wesley uses the language of "going on to perfection." Jesus uses the language of going on to completion (*teleios*). The Bible uses a variety of images used to communicate this movement:

- Undertaking a journey (3 John 6-7)
- Coming home (Zephaniah 3:20)
- Putting on the armor of light (Romans 13:12)
- Putting on the armor of God (Ephesians 6:11-12)
- Running the race. (Hebrews 12:1)

You will observe that for each of the dimensions of growth we have discussed, common to each dimension is a recurrent theme of movement towards transformation. This is the act of *becoming* that is the natural state of the disciple. The defining characteristic of this revolutionary movement from our old selves towards God's ideal is that we are focused less and less on ourselves – our needs, our desires, our struggles – and more and more on the needs, desires, and struggles of others. At the same time, we are finding more and more of ourselves surrendered to the will of God for our lives and discovering the joy of intimacy with the One who created us.

Discipleship is not about us and what we get from the deal. It is about how we are becoming like the One who, in every dimension of His being, was continually focused on others, sacrificing Himself in every way in every moment to the service of others.

SECTION 4

How Disciples Develop

Clear vision/expectations

Most congregations expect people to attend a "membership class" before they can join. Most commonly, this class runs between two and four hours and includes the following:

- An introduction to the pastor, staff, and key leaders
- An overview of the ministries of the church and explanation of how the church can serve those becoming members
- A brief history of the congregation/church
- An introduction to the history of the denomination with core beliefs
- And (of course) a pledge card for financial commitments.

In a church culture where it is all about getting people involved in the church and keeping people happy in the church, this all makes sense. This is a scenario being lived out in congregations across the country. Our membership emphasis has become more about joining and feeling at home in our club, rather than expecting members to grow as disciples of Jesus and providing them with the tools to pursue this goal.

By the way, when I read our mission statement, none of this misidentification of priorities makes much sense. Consider the words of Jesus:

> *Therefore go and make disciples of all nations, baptizing them in the name of the Father and of the Son and of the Holy Spirit, and teaching them to obey everything I have commanded you*
>
> **Matthew 28:19–20 (NRSV)**

Or the mission statement of The United Methodist Church:

To make disciples of Jesus Christ for the transformation of the world.

The church exists to "make disciples," not just members. So, what's the difference?

Consider the following table and the distinctions made:

Members	Mature Disciples
Goal: Get people to join the congregation.	Goal: Create disciples who are increasing in their love of God and neighbor.
Church Role: Keep the members satisfied.	Church Role: Provide opportunities and relationships to foster spiritual growth.
Leadership Role: Encourage members to be involved in church activities.	Leadership Role: Encourage disciples to grow in obedience to God and service to others.
Responsibility for Growth: Church (pastor, paid staff) assumes primary responsibility for motivating people in their spiritual journey.	Responsibility for Growth: Disciples assume primary responsibility for spiritual growth as the church provides opportunities and encouragement.

One of the significant lessons I learned about halfway through my work as a "real pastor" (serving in a local congregation) was that to live out our mission (to make disciples), requires a shift in focus from membership to discipleship. Membership says, "It's about me." Discipleship says, "It's about God and others."

The membership class described previously does little to cast a clear vision for growing as disciples. We have found that a focus on foundational spiritual practices and discernment of gifting for service is a more helpful approach.

A growing number of congregations are also finding it helpful to clearly articulate expectations around the themes of maturing discipleship. They have found that the traditional vows fall short of this clarity. Notice in the chart below how the Membership Covenant provides much more clarity in the expectations of the vows.

Traditional Vows	Dimensions of Discipleship	Membership Covenant
Prayers	Opening to Jesus/ Obeying Jesus	Participate regularly in a small discipleship group or other accountable discipling relationship.
Presence	A Life of Worship	Participate in weekly worship at least 3 weekends each month unless prevented by illness or travel.
Gifts	A Life of Generosity	Commit to proportional giving to the ministries of this congregation and to moving toward a tithe.
Service	A Life of Service	Serve in some way in the local community (beyond the walls of the church) each month.
Witness	A Life of Hospitality	Invite someone to come with me to church/events at least three times per year and build at least three relationships outside the church to witness the love of Christ.

Now notice the difference in the five words offered in the vow and a much-more clarifying membership covenant. Here is an example of a Membership Covenant:

Membership Covenant

I,_______________, trusting Jesus Christ as my Lord and Savior, seeking to be led by the Holy Spirit, and being in agreement with the mission and vision of Evergreen Church, as a part of the United Methodist Church, now desire to unite with the Evergreen Church family. In doing so, I commit myself to God and to the other members to do the following:

As we ***experience*** *God, I will strengthen the integrity of my church*

...by lovingly pursuing important personal relationships with other members (1 Peter 1:22)

...by refusing to participate in gossip or other negative conversation (Ephesians 4:29)

...by actively encouraging participation in Home Groups (Acts 2:42, 46)

...by living a godly life in response to God's grace (Micah 6:8; 1 John 2:6).

As we ***exalt*** *God, I will share in the joyful responsibility of my church*

...by attending faithfully with a heart ready for sincere worship (Hebrews 10:25)

...by being open-minded in worship, more committed to Spirit & truth than to comfort & tradition (John 4:23)

...by warmly welcoming those who visit (Romans 15:7)

...by praying for its faithfulness and growth (1 Samuel 12:23; 1 Thess. 1:1-2).

As we ***extend*** *God to others, I will serve Christ in the world through the ministry of my church*

...by discovering my gifts and talents (1 Peter 4:10) and being equipped to serve others (Ephesians 4)

...by seeking to have and live from a servant's heart (Philippians 2:3-7)

...by giving regularly to God through the church (Leviticus 27:30; 1 Corinthians 16:2)

...by inviting those without a church to attend worship with me (Luke 14:23).

The membership covenant emphasizes the relationship on the *commitment* to grow as disciples. The covenant agreement adds some "meat to the bones," clarifying how expectations were related to the vows taken by members of that specific congregation.

The Gallup organization, reporting their research done with faith communities in *Growing An Engaged Church,* notes:

Members need to know what is expected of them if they are to develop a strong sense of belonging within their congregation. Clarifying expectations creates a sense of stability, assuring members that they are valued. . . . 'A clear set of expectations is one of the ways members know they are receiving something of value from their congregation. . . .

So the very first thing you, as leaders, must do to ensure congregational effectiveness is to clarify membership expectations. What do you want your members' lives to look like – what is the fruit they should bear as a result of being planted in the soil of your church? What kinds of behaviors are consistent with being a member of your church? Do you want your members to be involved in community service projects? What about the frequency of attendance? Should your members be involved in some kind of study, growth, or support group? What do you expect in terms of financial support… ?

These are all questions you can answer by laying out clear membership expectations. Clear expectations lay the foundation for everything else your congregation is called to do and be. Without them, members will drift – eventually, right out the door.[13]

[13] Albert Winseman, *Growing An Engaged Church*, Gallup Press, 2007.

SECTION FIVE

Discipleship as a Journey

The Apostle Paul urges us to grow into maturity or completeness. John Wesley uses the language of "Christian Perfection."

Whichever way we look at it, from the very beginning, discipleship has been a journey toward the fullness of life that is offered to us in Jesus Christ. This journey happens in stages of development, very similar to our life stages. In fact, this is the very language that Jim Putman uses in *Real Life Discipleship*:[14]

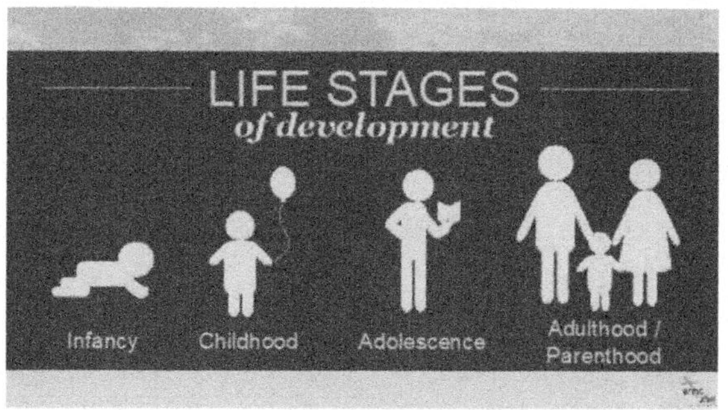

[14] Jim Putnam, *Real Life Discipleship*, NavPress, 2010.

It doesn't take a lot of imagination to see the connections to the journey in faith. In infancy, we are exploring everything. The whole world is new, and we're amazed by what we're experiencing. But we're not really engaged, except to serve our role as cute and cuddly centers of attention.

In the childhood phase, we are totally into learning about our world. We don't know much, if anything, and someone has to guide us along – teach us the language, keep us from doing things that will hurt us, and help us to develop in ways that will be the foundations for the rest of life.

The adolescent phase moves us into taking responsibility for our lives. We begin to establish some independence. We discover what works well for us. We make some of our own decisions about how to do life.

The parenthood/adult phase moves us squarely into the realm of focusing beyond ourselves. We realize that life done well is done so by helping others do life well. We continue to grow personally, but the focus becomes other-centered.

We use the language of Searching, Exploring, Beginning, Growing, and Maturing to describe these phases of development as a disciple:

PHASES OF DISCIPLESHIP: *Growing in Christ*

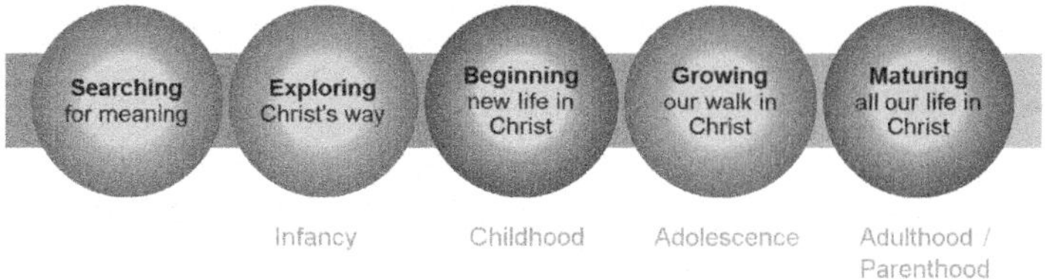

The phases might be described as:

***Searching** (pre-life in Christ):* All persons seek to make sense of their life, asking questions like, "What gives my life purpose, joy, and fulfillment?" They may seek to fill this fundamental need in many different ways. (See Acts 17:22.)

***Exploring** (infancy):* May attend church and want to belong, but they have not yet committed to following Jesus. They may wrestle intellectually with God's presence in their life, often with more caution than curiosity. The longer they attend without moving beyond this phase. However, the less likely they are to commit. (See John 1:45.)

***Beginning** (childhood):* Growing to understand and put their newfound faith into practice. Growth can be awkward. They are often vulnerable to insecurity and doubt. They are also the most excited about their faith. This is the largest and most active segment in church activities. (See Matthew 7:24.)

***Growing** (adolescent):* Eager to be identified as Christians and going public with their faith. They are increasingly willing to take responsibility for their deepening relationship with Jesus. They seek to integrate their faith into life in a holistic way and look to Jesus to help them live their life. (See Ephesians 4:14.)

***Maturing** (parents):* This group is moving toward complete surrender of their lives to Jesus. They exist to know, love, obey, serve, and be with Jesus. They also realize that the role of a disciple is to help make other disciples and live life with that focus. (See Galatians 2:20.)

It is important to note here that not only are there phases of development and that people in the congregation will find themselves in different phases, but also that the various dimensions of the life of a disciple will often reflect differing levels of maturity. For example, a person may have a great passion for serving others and a well-developed sense of calling (maturing phase for service) but may be in the beginning phase for opening to Jesus. They have made a commitment to be a disciple but have not moved into a growing relationship. Often the service dimension can serve as a catalyst for growth in other areas.

A friend of mine (we'll call him Jack) is an American contractor who lives in another country where he runs a construction business. Jack and I got connected through a seemingly obscure relational link through a mission organization (ReGenesis Ministries), for which I provided leadership. Jack is what one might describe as "a little rough around the edges" (maybe a lot!). He is a lapsed Catholic and a former drug addict.

Yet, every time I take a mission team to that area, Jack takes the week off from his business and arranges supplies for the project, provides equipment for the team, and even trains the team for the project's needs. During those team experiences, Jack also goes to church, attends daily devotional times, makes sure that we pray for every meal, and announces to everybody we meet, "This is my preacher friend from the States."

Jack is a perfect example of a more developed person in one area than in another. We suggest that you build on the strengths. With Jack, it took several trips before he began to respond to anything "spiritual" or "religious." Over the years, he has come a long way. Now, he even invites his friends to go to church with him.

It is also important to note that we are never finished growing, maturing, developing, and transforming as disciples. There is always more to discover, learn, and experience as a disciple. This is not a linear process with a beginning and an end. Rather is it an ever-evolving journey of pursuing and growing more Christ-like. Too often, church members interpret their full maturity as a disciple since they have taken "all the classes," held all the offices, or been involved in all the ministries. Maturing in our discipleship and discipling others is never completed on this side of heaven.

Relational Support for the Discipleship Process

Discipleship happens in relationships! I'm not sure why, but we seem to have moved away from this understanding and substituted an educational model rather than focusing on the relational aspects of discipleship and supplementing them with solid Christian education.

Jesus didn't say, "Take a class." He said, "Come, follow me." Discipleship is personal and relational.

The genius of John Wesley, founder of the Methodist movement, was that of building a process for discipleship based on different levels of relationship. The following diagram depicts that process:

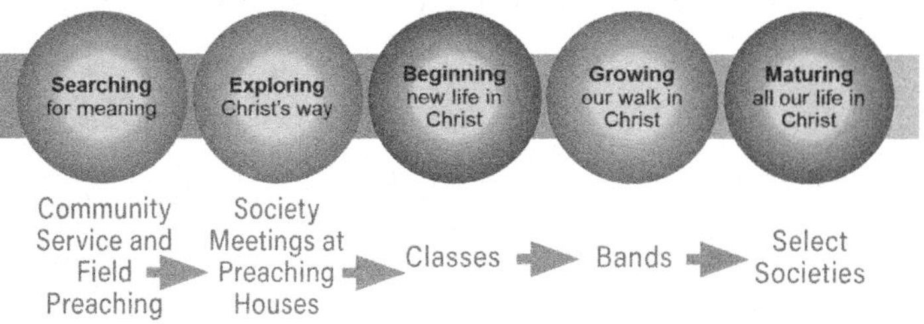

When people were exploring the faith, they were invited to a society meeting (basically a worship service) where they could understand why it was important to be a disciple of Jesus.

As persons began their commitment as a disciple of Jesus, they were required to participate (if they wanted to be Methodists) in a Class Meeting. This was a larger group format led by a spiritual leader with weekly meetings designed to teach the basics of the faith and hold people accountable for their progress in living as disciples.

The most mature members of the Class Meeting group were invited to participate in Bands. These were much smaller groups (four or five people of the same gender) who engaged, under the leadership of a spiritual coach, in a much more intense focus on faith training and accountability.

The best of the Bands were selected for one-on-one training in faith development and leadership, and were prepared to become leaders of Societies, Classes, and Bands.

Churches that do disciple well use this same type of framework for the flow of a discipleship pathway. They recognize that people at different places along the developmental pathway have different needs in the type of relational support offered and training provided. The following chart provides some insights into what works best at each phase of development.

Phase	Wesley's Process	Contemporary Applications	Relational/ Educational
Searching	Community Service and Field Preaching	Attractional events, building relationships, & community service	NA
Exploring	Society Meetings – Preaching Houses (worship)	Corporate worship (small groups and service opportunities are also great connecting points)	One-on-one relational connections with guests/visitors.
Beginning	Class Meeting – training in basic Christian practices	Foundations Class: Spiritual Practices and Christian Beliefs	Teacher/Facilitator Mentors could be used in place of a class
Growing	Bands – deep accountable relationships building maturity in living life as a disciple in all dimensions	Small Groups providing training and accountability	Small Groups and Discipleship Coaches Training and development around dimensions of discipleship in core curriculum
Maturing	Select Societies – equipping leaders to become Society Preachers, Class Leaders, Band Leaders, Ministry Leaders	Very small groups/ one-on-one training for Leadership	Apprentices Mentors Discipleship Coaches Spiritual Directors

Connecting and Developing a Core Curriculum

A friend recently admitted that if anyone in his church became a maturing disciple of Jesus, it was strictly by accident. I think this may be more of a reality in many of our churches than we would like to admit.

It is a fairly common scenario when I consult with local congregations about discipleship, to be handed a flyer or brochure listing all the opportunities for people to participate in a class during the next "semester." The classes include a wide variety of topics. Many are offered because someone suggested a great new book or one of the contemporary well-known pastors/authors just released a new talking head series.

Little thought is given to "keeping the end in mind" (to use a well-worn Stephen Covey phrase). Yet, this is exactly where we need to start. What does a maturing disciple of Jesus do? How does the church help equip disciples to live in this manner? For example, if maturity as we describe it for a life of generosity means that we live on less than God provides (creating financial margins) so that we can bless others more, we will probably need to move beyond just telling people that this is what we hope for them. In a culture with rampant consumerism and materialism, the church needs to help people discover a countercultural mindset where they find their worth in God and not stuff. In a culture where people live paycheck to paycheck, regularly extending themselves beyond their means, the church has an opportunity to help people learn how to handle their finances in a biblical manner. Only then can disciples begin to live into maturity in a life of generosity.

We need to start with a vision for maturing discipleship and then provide the training to help people live into the vision. I suggest this happens when we intentionally design a core curriculum and set the expectation that all participants in the church will engage in this process. That core curriculum might look something like this:

Beginning Phase: A foundational course (could be the membership class) where all participants are introduced to basic theological concepts and foundational spiritual practices.

Growing Phase: Classes specific to each of the dimensions of discipleship in which you are encouraging maturity.

- A Life of Worship
- A Life of Hospitality
- A Life Opening to Jesus
- A Life Obeying Jesus
- A Life of Service
- A Life of Generosity.

The following are some possible resources that you might find helpful:

Beginning Phase

***A Disciple's Path*, by Jim Harnish.** This resource provides a strong introduction to the basic elements of the life of a disciple, focusing on prayers, presence, gifts, service, and witness.

***Foundations*, by Phil Maynard.** This resource provides an introduction to spiritual practices, including how to have a devotional time, how to read the Bible, how to pray, how to explore giftedness in serving, how to use financial resources faithfully, and how to share your faith.

***Alpha*, by Nicky Gumble.** An introduction to basic Christian beliefs and practices engaged through table conversation in a small group setting.

Growing Phase

(The core curriculum optimally offers a minimum of one study for each dimension of the six dimensions of discipleship: worship, hospitality, opening to Jesus, obedience, service, and generosity.)

A LIFE OF WORSHIP

***Holy Roar*, by Chris Tomlin and Darren Whitehead.** This study, themed around seven words for worship, is designed to deepen our understanding and worship practice.

***The Unquenchable Worshiper,* by Matt Redmon.** A brief book by songwriter Matt Redmon is about living a devoted life in the presence of God.

A LIFE OF HOSPITALITY

***Making Room,* by Christine Pohl.** A deep reflection on the Christian tradition of hospitality, explored through both historical research and contemporary communities.

***Connect!,* by Phil Maynard.** A practical guide to living out hospitality in our churches, neighborhoods, circles of influence, and communities.

***Authentic Community,* by Jim Van Yperen.** A strong exploration of authentic community through the "one anothers" found in the Bible.

A LIFE OPENING TO JESUS

***Companions in Christ,* available through Upper Room Ministries.** A wonderful overview of spiritual practices explored through engagement in a small group setting.

***Celebration of Discipline,* by Richard Foster.** A classic work on spiritual practices by one of the leading practitioners of spiritual disciplines.

***Devotion Life in the Wesleyan Tradition*, by Steve Harper.** A good overview of spiritual practices traditionally engaged by Methodists through the ages.

A LIFE OBEYING JESUS

***Eat This Book*, by Eugene Peterson**. An introduction to the practice of engaging Scripture through spiritual reading.

***A Reflective Life*, by Ken Gire**. The practices of reading the moment, reflecting on the moment, and responding to the moment, applied to Scripture and life.

Disciple Bible Study. A 32-week guide through the writings of both the Hebrew Scriptures and the New Testament.

***Discipler*, by Phil Maynard**. A relational, intentional, and accountable guide to the discovery of practices and understandings that lead to spiritual maturity.

A LIFE OF SERVICE

***SHAPE*, by Eric Rees**. Using the SHAPE framework (spiritual gifts, heart, abilities, personality, and life experiences), the author guides an experience of discovering how God has wired each person for service.

***The Externally Focused Church*, by Rick Rusaw and Eric Swanson**. This book brings to focus the call to service as the identifying mark of Christians and the Church.

A LIFE OF GENEROSITY

***Financial Peace*, by Dave Ramsey**. A wonderful study in the biblical principles of financial management that will transform the understanding of how to use resources.

***Enough*, by Adam Hamilton**. In a world struggling with stress, anxiety, and fear due to financial struggles, the author points out that Jesus directs us to another path.

***Earn, Save, Give: Wesley's Simple Rules for Money*, by Jim Harnish**. In this brief work, Harnish translates John Wesley's teachings on money into a personal faith experience for the 21st century.

Maturing Phase

The training for this phase of development would be focused around leadership development and might include courses in discipleship coaching, mentoring, leading teams, administrative teams, etc.

SECTION SIX

Creating a Discipleship Pathway

Journey of Grace

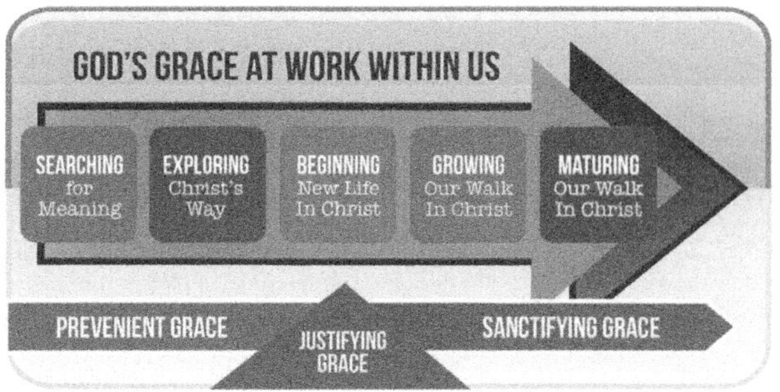

Previously, we have looked at how the phases of discipleship growth parallel all humans' physical and mental development. Growth as a disciple, however, is not an autonomous process that organically proceeds heedless of conscious management on our part. Growth as a follower of Jesus Christ is a matter of will, decision, and effort.

We have discussed some of the relational infrastructure that is helpful to facilitate this growth, and we have explored some of the educational support that equips disciples to make life transformation happen. But we have talked about all of this in language that makes it seem like "making disciples" is something WE (the church) do. This is only natural since we have denominational mission statements like:

> *Make disciples of Jesus Christ for the transformation of the world.*
>
> **The United Methodist Book of Discipline**

And even the words of Jesus in the Great Commission:

> *Go, therefore, and make disciples . . . baptizing them . . . and teaching them. . .*
>
> **Matthew 28: 19-20 (NRSV)**

However, the reality is that we (the church) do not really make disciples. God makes disciples. We provide the framework, the opportunities, the relationships, and the educational resources to support what God is doing. But it is God who makes disciples. It is God at work through Prevenient Grace – the working of the Spirit of God to woo us, draw us in, invite us – that introduces us to the relationship of being a disciple. It is God at work through Justifying Grace – the working of the Spirit of God to place us in a relationship where we are justified (made right with God) that we experience imputed righteousness (God's choice to see us as righteous). And it is God at work through Sanctifying Grace – the working of the Spirit of God in our lives to impart (make actual) the righteousness of Christ – through which we journey toward *Christian Perfection* or completeness.

With that clarified (and in the spirit of Paul's admonition to "work out your salvation"), there is much we as the church can and should do to make the pathway to maturity as a disciple as navigable as possible. Throughout history, there have been a few processes that stand out as exceptional.

Biblical Approaches to Discipleship

The Jesus Approach

One of the best descriptions of this approach to discipleship is a video segment by Rob Bell. It is part of the Nooma Series and is entitled "Dust." You can watch this video on YouTube by searching the site for "Rob Bell, dust." While you may or may not agree entirely with Bell's theology, this video highlights a model of discipleship practiced in the time of Jesus that changed the world as it was known.

The educational system for Jewish children focused on the memorization of scriptures, with greater and greater portions of Scripture memorized as students advanced into their teenage years. At that point most of these students would return to learning a trade by working in the family business. A select few, those with the clearest aptitude for this kind of training, would apply to be a disciple of a rabbi (teacher). The rabbi would have conversations with them inspired by the scriptures and the interpretation of scriptures known as the *Midrash*. If the student were exceptional, and the rabbi thought they had potential, they would advance further. The best of the best were selected to be disciples. These students would leave their homes, their families, and their communities to follow the rabbi. Wherever the rabbi went and whatever the rabbi did, the students would follow closely in the rabbi's footsteps, taking on the character and developing the skills of the rabbi.

Hence, a saying of blessing was developed for these students: "May you be covered in the dust of your rabbi."

Jesus followed this pattern for making disciples with one very important distinction. The people he invited to be disciples had already returned to their families and were already engaged in the family trade by the time Jesus came along and said, "Come, follow me." The implication is clear. You don't have to be the best of the best in academic performance. We can be a disciple of Jesus when the heart is in the right place. It is possible for each of us to become more like Jesus and to do the things Jesus did. But this doesn't happen by accident. Greg Ogden, in *Transforming Discipleship,* examines the discipleship approach of Jesus. The following graphic summarizes that process: [15]

	Pre disciple (Seeking)	Phase I (Exploring)	Phase II (Beginning)	Phase III (Growing)	Phase IV (Maturing)
Jesus' Role	*Inviter*	*Living Example*	*Provocative Teacher*	*Supportive Coach*	*Ultimate Delegator*
The Disciples' Role	*Seekers*	*Observers & Imitators*	*Students & Questioners*	*Short Term Missionaries*	*Apostles*
Readiness Level	*Hungry to know about Messiah*	*Ready to observe who Jesus is*	*Ready to interact & identify with Jesus*	*Ready to test the authority of Jesus*	*Ready to assume full responsibility*
Key Question	*Is Jesus Messiah?*	*Is Jesus Messiah?*	*What is the cost of following Jesus?*	*Will the power of Jesus work in me?*	*Will I give my life to the disciple making mission?*

15 Greg Ogden, *Transforming Discipleship,* IVP Books, 2003.

You will note that Ogden's framework is similar to the phases of development highlighted in our earlier sections. He identifies five phases of development, but his descriptions are a bit more generic than those we developed, so I have included our familiar terminology in parentheses under his phases on the graphic. Let's consider the various components of this approach:

- ***The Disciples' role:*** Notice the movement from the left side of the graphic to the right as disciples move from checking out what it means to be a disciple (observers and imitators) to learning what to do as disciples (students) to beginning to develop the *how* of applying this new lifestyle (short term missionaries) to fully representing Christ to the world (apostles). It is a shift from us (and our development) to a focus on the world and how we can make a difference in it – very similar to the *Real Discipleship* matrix presented previously.
- ***Jesus's role:*** In a fashion similar to considering the role of the church in making disciples, Jesus starts out as Inviter (incarnational hospitality), moves to being the Example (the witness of the church), becomes the Teacher (providing training), moves to being the Supportive Coach (helps

disciples see how to live out their calling), and then becomes delegator (sending maturing disciples out to be Christ in the world).

- Even the questions Ogden identifies are similar to concepts we have previously considered:
  - Why? (Is Jesus the Messiah?)
  - What? (What is the cost?)
  - How? (Will the power of Jesus work in me?)
  - What if? (Will I give my life to the disciple-making mission?)

Paul's Approach

Ogden identified a different but very similar approach used by the Apostle Paul and represented in the following graphic: [16]

The Apostle Paul's Process

Life Stage	Life Stage Role	Disciples Role	Paul's Role
Infancy	Modeling and direction	Imitation	Model
Childhood	Unconditional love and protection	Identification	Hero
Adolescence	Increased freedom and identity formation	Exhortation	Coach
Adulthood	Mutuality and reciprocity	Participation	Peer

Adapted from Transforming Discipleship, Greg Ogden

[16] Greg Ogden, *Transforming Discipleship,* IVP Books, 2003.

Ogden shows how Paul emulates Jesus's example. Note in particular:

- ***The Disciples' role:*** Starting with imitation (the infancy phase), the disciples watch and learn from those who are more mature; then they move to identification (the childhood phase), where they begin to form life around teachings; they grow from there to exhortation (the adolescence phase), in which the disciples are encouraged and given the freedom to use what they are becoming; and ultimately they arrive at participation (the adulthood phase) in which the disciples realize their goal of full partnership in building the kingdom

- ***Paul's role:*** Paul starts out as a model, moves to hero (in the sense of being looked up to), serves as coach (supporting the disciples as they serve), and ultimately becomes a peer to his fellow, fully engaged disciples.

The Early Church's Approach to Discipleship

In Christianity, during the first couple of centuries, there were very clear expectations and a three-year process of development/ probation period for those being admitted into the church as disciples of Jesus Christ. This included instruction by a mentor for about two years focused around the *Didache* materials (a discipleship program that eventually became known as *The Training of the Lord through the Twelve Apostles to the Gentiles*).[17]

The process for admission into the Christian community had several steps:

- Recommendation of a present member vouching for the authenticity of faith.
- Three-year probation period.
- Doctrinal and moral training (during three-year probation).
- Examination of knowledge and conduct.
- Training in the scriptures.
- Initiation into spiritual practices.
- Baptism.
- Acceptance into the community and celebration of Holy Communion.

Can you imagine a church that required a three-year process for membership in our culture today?

---

[17] Marcia Ford, *Traditions of the Ancients*, B&H Publishing Group, 2006.

I have worked with a fair number of churches that have no process at all. At the end of worship, an invitation is extended: "If you would like to join this congregation today, simply come forward during our closing hymn." And then, they are asked to respond to the membership vows.

This is a reasonable approach if your goal is to get members on the rolls and have your church look really healthy for those who admire spreadsheets. It is not a great metric for measurement if your goal is making disciples.

It is a blind invitation – open and accessible, true, but generic in the sense that it does not meet the person with a sense of expectation of discipleship maturation or guiding them on their highly personal journey of discipleship.

You know nothing about the man or woman who steps forward on the seventh verse of "Just as I Am." You don't know if they have been baptized. You don't know if they have been a member of a church somewhere else, where they are on the pathway to maturity as a disciple, or what level of commitment they have to the life and ministry of your local congregation.

The Early Methodists' Discipleship Approach

Several years ago, Eric Geiger (co-author of the book, *Simple Church)* was presenting a series of workshops in the Florida Conference of The United Methodist Church around the *Simple Church* themes. As a Conference staff person, I was responsible for getting Eric to the locations where he would be speaking. As we were driving into Gainesville for an event, Eric turned to me and asked the question: "Phil, I just have one question. What's wrong with you people?"

My initial response was that he would have to be more specific. I could think of a lot of answers to that question. Then, he said: "I work with pastors and church leaders from a wide variety of tribes [denomination/non-denominational traditions]. All of them are using the best discipleship process since the time of Jesus – the one developed by John Wesley and the early Methodists. Everybody, that is, but the Methodists. What's wrong with you people?"

I didn't have an answer.

What was so special about the discipleship approach of John Wesley? The following graphic provides insight:

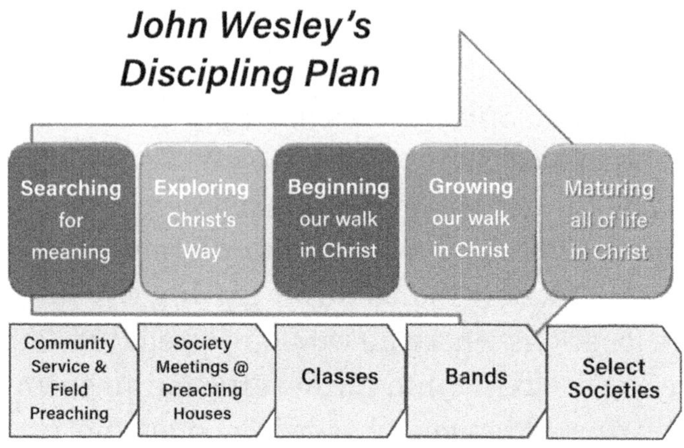

John Wesley and the early Methodists, first and foremost, had a heart for the community – for people outside the church. The covenant they ascribed to included serving people in some way each week. The Methodist preachers were known for bringing the message of the gospel to those outside of the church, preaching at the mines and the inner cities, and even in cemeteries. John Wesley penned the words in his journal that became a theme of his ministry and the theme of Methodism as the movement grew. He wrote, "I look upon all the world as my parish. [It is] my bounden duty to declare to all who are willing to hear, the glad tidings of salvation."[18]

---

[18] See *The Journal of John Wesley*, Christian Classics Ethereal Library, www.ccel.org

People were drawn to the gospel of Christ through the lives of those called Methodists (which was, by the way, a derogatory designation critiquing the strong focus on *methods*, such as committing to serve someone each week, studying the scriptures every day, and praying for family and friends). The Methodists cared for the sick, visited those in prison, fed the hungry, and clothed the poor. It seems there was something about being the witness of Christ in the world that drew people to the love of Jesus for themselves. Some of the people who experienced God's grace through their interactions with these so-called Methodists asked how they could learn more. At this point in their spiritual journey, they were invited to Wesley's Society Meeting.

A Society Meeting had all the elements of what we would call a worship service today. There were prayers, hymns, scripture readings, sermons, the sacrament of communion, and altar calls. The underlying message of the teaching time was "the desire to flee from the wrath to come." It was an invitation to discipleship framed in a rather negative context that would not be well received in contemporary culture. But it was culturally relevant for its time, and thus effective, in Wesley's time.

Some of those drawn to Society Meetings by the acts of mercy performed by Methodists would inquire about how to move into this saving relationship with Jesus Christ and, in particular, how to become Methodists. The answer went something like this: "You can become a Methodist only if you commit to be part of a Class Meeting. You can become a Christian by going to church and giving your life to Christ. But to be a Methodist, you have to join a Class Meeting." The Class Meeting was where one learned how to live as a disciple of Jesus Christ.

The Class Meeting was not just informational. It was transformational. Based on my research, this is how I envision the class meetings of the time. Each "class" was led by a Class Leader – a maturing disciple of Jesus Christ. The gathering was formed around a Covenant of Discipleship. The class members were accountable for their development as disciples based on living into the covenant agreement. (A contemporary version of that covenant was introduced earlier on building the infrastructure of discipling relationships.)

As the class leader asked each member about their faithfulness to the covenant components, an opportunity was provided for teaching, encouragement, and support. For example, if a member confessed that he/she was having difficulty living into the part of the covenant related to personal Bible study ("study the scriptures each day according to a plan"), the Class Leader or the Class might talk about what plan the member was trying to follow, how the plan might be adjusted to make it more workable, what obstacles might remain for living into the plan, and what the member would commit to doing for the next week.

In other words, it was pretty much like a group coaching situation.

Those who excelled in their growth as disciples through the Class Meeting were invited to participate in a Band (the next level of development). There were Men's Bands and Women's Bands. The level of accountability and vulnerability increased exponentially in the Band. For example, instead of talking about how to develop a plan for reading the scriptures, the focus would be on specific temptations the Band members were dealing with and how to overcome them and remain faithful.

As I have workshop participant role-play participants using these materials, I usually pick someone that doesn't seem to embarrass easily. Then I explain: In a Band meeting, the focus was on "fleeing from the wrath to come." Now, this is not a popular message in our day, but in Wesley's time, it proved very effective. So, the Bandleader might say to a participant: "Tom, we exist to help each other flee from the wrath to come through God's Grace. The Evil One is doing everything in his power to draw us away from our commitment. We are constantly being tempted to live in a way that is inconsistent with the life we have been called to live. Sometimes it is to seek forbidden pleasures, or to think more highly of ourselves than others, or to judge others, or to engage in the use of substances that are immoral. Would you stand and share with the group all the ways you have been tempted over the past week, so that we can encourage you to stand firm?"

Of course, the response is something like, "You don't really have time for my list!" And we all have a good laugh. But for those in the Bands it was no laughing matter. This sin stuff was serious.

The final level of discipleship in the Wesleyan model was the invitation to participate in a Select Society. Here the "best of the best" were invited to engage in personal relationships or very small groups for their development as leaders in the Methodist Movement. They were equipped to become Class Meeting Leaders, Band Leaders, Society Leaders, and Preachers in the Methodist movement. In the interest of complete transparency, there were two types of Select Societies, the one just described and the one no disciple wanted to be invited to. The second of these was focused on remedial training. It was for those disciples who had failed to live into a lifestyle reflecting that of the movement. It was for "backsliders."

Wesley's model is still the most successful approach to discipleship in our time. So, let's explore how everything we have talked about is reflected in that model.

Visualizing the Flow of Wesley's Discipleship Process

Let's "begin with the end in mind," to again use the language of Stephen Covey. Wesley had clarity about what a Methodist disciple was supposed to be and do. It was summed up in two clearly articulated dimensions:

- Holiness of heart and life.
- Works of mercy.

In the dimension of **holiness of heart and life**, there were clearly articulated behaviors as represented in the graphic below:[19]

Spiritual Disciplines

doing good works, visiting the sick, visiting those in prison, feeding the hungry, and giving generously to the needs of others

seeking justice, ending oppression and discrimination, and addressing the needs of the poor

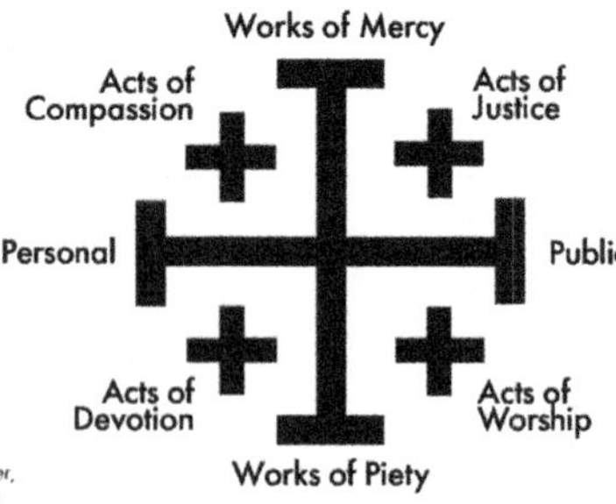

reading, meditating and studying the scriptures, prayer, fasting, regularly attending worship, healthy living, and sharing our faith with others

regularly share in the sacraments, Christian conferencing (accountability to one another), and Bible study

It is easy to see the way that these behaviors align with the dimensions of spiritual growth that we identified previously when we discussed clarity of vision:

A Life of Worship:

- ✓ The Public worship of God.
- ✓ The Lord's Supper.

---

[19] Adapted from the work of the Rev. Dr. Steve Manskar, *Forming Christian Disciples*, Published by Discipleship Resources, Nashville, TN

A Life of Hospitality:

- ✓ Christian conferencing.
- ✓ Welcoming the stranger.

A Life Opening to Jesus:

- ✓ Searching the scriptures.
- ✓ Family and private prayer.
- ✓ Christian conferencing.

A Life Obeying Jesus:

- ✓ Christian conferencing.
- ✓ Searching the scriptures.

A Life of Service:

- ✓ Care for the sick.
- ✓ Visiting the imprisoned.

A Life of Generosity:

- ✓ Feeding the hungry.
- ✓ Clothing the naked.
- ✓ Sheltering the homeless.

It was a people called Methodists who were living into a life of holiness and mercy (*growing and maturing in the faith)* that engaged a world that was ***searching*** for meaning in life. Through the lives they lived and the acts of service they offered, people beyond the walls of the church began to discover the love of Jesus Christ. These people were expressions of God's grace to a broken and hurting world. And while there were some notable exceptions, the primary Methodist witness was not actually the preacher at the mines, in the marketplace, or at the cemetery. The primary witness was the everyday Methodist disciple who lived life in accordance with a public commitment. They went to church and prayed and studied Scripture and served and were generous to those in need.

And people responded to these everyday disciples. They wanted to know more about this Jesus who could take ruffians like these and help them discover a "holiness of heart and life." Some of the people the disciples engaged even asked how to get that for themselves.

They were invited to begin ***exploring*** the faith by coming to a Society meeting. In that setting, they witnessed lives that had been changed by the power of God: they heard from people who talked about how God had provided for their greatest needs; they listened to how the scriptures could be applied to their lives; they prayed for the needs of the communities around them; they experienced the touch of the Holy One. Someone who was further along in the journey than they were had a conversation with them, answered their questions and walked with them as they decided if the disciple's life was the right thing for them. And some of them decided that this was what they wanted for their own lives. So, they asked what they had to do to be a disciple of Jesus like this.

And they got two answers.

First, if they wanted to be a disciple of Jesus, they could get involved in their local parish. They could go to church. They could become active participants in mission and ministry. After all, Wesley never intended to set up another denomination. In a strong sense, the Methodist movement was a parachurch movement designed to meet a need not being met by the traditional church.

Second, if people were interested in ***beginning*** a relationship with Jesus through the Methodists, the next step was to become part of a Class Meeting. While this was not a **class** in the modern sense of someone presenting information (lecturer/facilitator) to participants sitting in a circle making copious notes in their workbooks or Bibles. Instead, it was a class in the sense of a great deal of instruction taking place, with the practice of key principles being engaged and accountability for personal application being standard fare. This is where the foundations of the faith were built, theology discussed, and spiritual practices formed. The role of the class leader in this setting included coaching and mentoring those who were assigned to his or her care. They even collected an offering and made time for one-on-one personalized conversations.

For those in the class meetings who were ***growing*** as disciples, demonstrating lifestyle and behavioral changes reflecting the vision for a people called Methodists, they were invited to be part of a Band or a **small group** where they continued to learn how to live more fully into the fullness of a relationship with Jesus and faithful witness to the world. In the Bands, the participants dug deep, learning how to live as maturing disciples of Jesus. The "best of the best" in the Bands were invited to participate in Select Societies where the ***maturing*** disciples were equipped through even smaller groups and one-on-one relationships to become leaders in the Methodist movement – preachers, teachers, class meeting leaders, and band leaders.

Wesley was brilliant! The flow of a discipling process he birthed is the hallmark of the most successful discipleship processes in a variety of traditions today. The non-denominational churches are doing this particularly well. So, for those of us who have yet to establish an accessible, structured framework for our own discipleship process, what would such a process look like? Let's begin with the end in mind one more time.

Clarity of purpose and goals

Bringing together the examples of the early church, the wisdom of centuries, and best practices gleaned from modern congregations, we have defined a clear set of expectations for the characteristics that define the lifestyle of a maturing disciple.

Maturing disciples will:

- Live lives honoring God in the ways they work, play, and engage others.
- Intentionally build relationships in order to be Christ to someone.

- Take responsibility for their own spiritual growth.
- Disciple someone else, helping them move toward maturity.
- Use their gifts and talents to serve others.
- Live within margins in order to bless others.

Let's summarize all we have learned from previous chapters about the dimensions of discipleship and the healthy progress from phase to phase:

> To engage people in the ***searching*** phase, disciples from the beginning, growing, and maturing phases build relationships with the ultimate purpose of being Christ in the lives of others whom they encounter. That may include simply being a good friend, a helpful neighbor, a companion in the workplace, or serving a need. And some of those people, having seen Christ's love shine through these disciples, may respond by seeking a relationship with God like the one to which their lives bear witness.
>
> For those who are ***exploring*** the faith – perhaps because of one of the disciples described in the previous paragraph – it is helpful for someone

to join them on the journey. They probably know little about the Christian faith. Or, if they do have some prior connection to Christianity, it may have been a negative experience. Having someone to talk with, ask questions, and explore possibilities with is the need. Some churches have sponsors or mentors, or coaches that fill this role.

For those making a clear commitment to be a disciple, ***beginning*** the journey creates a profound need to know what is expected of them and to be given instruction in the basics of the faith and introductory spiritual practices. A class setting is probably the least intimidating way to accomplish this. For smaller churches, providing mentors who could walk alongside the new believer is a viable option. This is also the point at which expectations are clearly articulated (e.g., membership covenant, baptism, etc.).

For those ***growing*** a deeper relationship with Christ, the greatest need is to understand how to live more fully into the life God has offered. This is the time when a variety of educational opportunities are provided to help growing disciples apply the teachings of Jesus to real life. This application of wisdom and habits is greatly enhanced with access to the appropriate type of supportive relationships (e.g., small groups, mentors, discipleship coaches). The typical disciple will spend a significant amount of time in this phase of development relative to the time in the exploring and beginning phases.

Those ***maturing*** in the faith will always need continuing support in the form of a one-on-one relationship with a mentor, discipleship coach, or spiritual director. While maturing disciples have already formed the basic practices, habits, and lifestyles that reflect their level of faith, there is an ongoing need to pay attention to God at work in their lives and to be faithful (through accountability) to the disciplines necessary to continue deepening their relationship with the Creator. These persons have the maturity to move into leadership roles within their congregations with the proper training and apprenticing.

The following graphic is designed to visualize how all these elements of a Discipleship Pathway fit together:

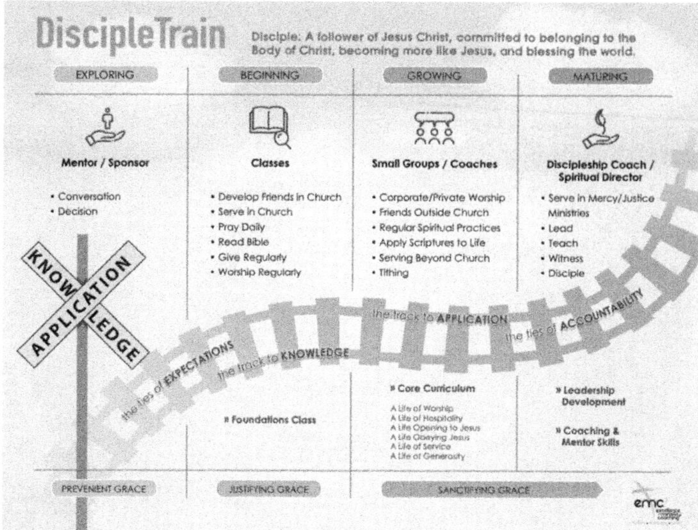
DiscipleTrain
Disciple: A follower of Jesus Christ, committed to belonging to the Body of Christ, becoming more like Jesus, and blessing the world.
EXPLORING
BEGINNING
GROWING
MATURING
Mentor / Sponsor
• Conversation
• Decision
Classes
• Develop Friends in Church
• Serve in Church
• Pray Daily
• Read Bible
• Give Regularly
• Worship Regularly
Small Groups / Coaches
• Corporate/Private Worship
• Friends Outside Church
• Regular Spiritual Practices
• Apply Scriptures to Life
• Serving Beyond Church
• Tithing
Discipleship Coach / Spiritual Director
• Serve in Mercy/Justice Ministries
• Lead
• Teach
• Witness
• Disciple
KNOWLEDGE
APPLICATION
the ties of EXPECTATIONS
the track to KNOWLEDGE
the track to APPLICATION
the ties of ACCOUNTABILITY
» Foundations Class
» Core Curriculum
A Life of Worship
A Life of Hospitality
A Life Opening to Jesus
A Life Obeying Jesus
A Life of Service
A Life of Generosity
» Leadership Development
» Coaching & Mentor Skills
PREVENIENT GRACE
JUSTIFYING GRACE
SANCTIFYING GRACE
emc

Questions for Conversation

What process is in place in your congregation to:

- Equip members/participants to build relationships with those outside the church (friends, neighbors, acquaintances, community)?

- Engage uncommitted persons exploring the faith to answer questions and discover the possibilities for life as a disciple of Jesus Christ?

- Train new believers in the basic theological understandings and spiritual practice that will serve as a foundation for the journey as a disciple?

- Provide growing disciples the tools, relationships, practices that will serve as catalysts for engaging the life as a disciple more fully?

- Build capacity as leaders for the congregation in growing maturing disciples, supporting the ministries of the church, and engaging the community?

- How does your church teach disciples to take responsibility for their own spiritual growth?

- What expectations are set for those serving in leadership within the congregation?

CONCLUSION

Tying It All Together

As you can see, there are many ways to look at discipleship. There is no one right way. Certainly, there are key elements as outlined that are recommended. Several effective models were offered for examination and consideration. Each church's discipleship process looks different. The most important thing to remember is that a church needs an intentional discipleship process in place. Without an intentional discipleship process/pathway, the church (or Expedition Team) will not be fulfilling the Great Commission. Disciples may enter into the process in a variety of ways (service, worship, community event) and entrance points depending on their discipleship journey thus far. Disciples progress or move in different ways and paces. The church needs an intentional process for developing disciples.

Here are some steps to consider as you begin to create your church's discipleship pathway:

1. Begin with the end in mind. What is it that a disciple would be, do, experience, demonstrate, practice, etc.? Describe a mature or maturing disciple.

2. What are the growth phases to include in the pathway (i.e., searching, exploring, beginning, growing, maturing)? Name the growth phases and define the meaning of each for clarity.

3. Next, identify key areas for concentrating growth and transformation in that particular phase. This could include things such as spiritual practices one is learning or routinely doing. This could outward signs and activities of a disciple.

4. Add other elements, phases, expectations to the discipleship pathway. This could be expectations of increased serving, leading, mentoring, coaching, accountability, etc.

5. Develop a discipleship covenant.

6. Create or identify any resources needed to help disciples engage in learning and growing in specific areas. Add the resource/class expectations to the discipleship pathway.

7. Create a visual representation of the pathway that is easily understood by the congregation, including how to engage and grow in the process.

8. Equip ministry team leaders, coaches, and mentors in the discipleship process. Invite ministry team leaders to create discipleship growth opportunities within their ministry areas. Help those participating in the ministries areas connect their ministry to the discipleship pathway.

9. Consider a sermon series to roll out the discipleship pathway to the congregation. Explain why the process is important, how to engage in the process, and the expectations for growth and transformation.

10. Help disciples connect the ministry offerings of the church to a step in their discipleship pathway.

Quotes From Other Books
in The Greatest Expedition Series

The multi-site movement keeps the church centered on God's consistent call to go and make disciples for the transformation of the world while staying connected to one another in community.

Ken Nash
Multi-Site Ministry

Stay flexible even when it is not easy. Due to the stress and responsibility of ministry, we can become rigid, pessimistic and fail to see the opportunities in front of us. A mark of great leadership is flexibility, being able to make adjustments when necessary.

Olu Brown
New Kind of Venture Leader

But let me be clear, we will not be making the case that online relationships and connections are the same as in-person ones; we all know they are not. But we will be talking about why online connections are valuable, and there is nothing "virtual" or "almost" about them.

Nicole Reilley
Digital Ministry

Quotes From Other Books
in The Greatest Expedition Series

While we find struggling churches in different contexts, theological backgrounds, sizes, and cultures, declining congregations have one thing in common: There is a palpable lack of focus on what God desires.

Jaye Johnson
Missional Accountability

How you think of your church will determine not only your priorities, but also your energy investment and actions. It will define how you lead and to what extent you live into what the church of Jesus Christ is intended to be.

Sue Nilson Kibbey
Open Road

Any collaboration with local people is a good thing – but the best collaboration is spiritual. It is where we begin to pray together about the community, and the emerging ministry. In such a spiritual collaboration, amazing things begin to happen.

Paul Nixon
Cultural Competency

What is *The Greatest Expedition*?

The Greatest Expedition is a congregational journey for churches, charges, or cooperative parishes led by a church Expedition Team of 8-12 brave pioneering leaders. The purpose of *The Greatest Expedition* is to provide an experience for Expedition Teams to explore their local context in new ways to develop new MAPS (ministry action plans) so you are more relevant and contextual to reach new people in your community. Updated tools and guides are provided for the church's Expedition Team. Yet, it is a "choose your own adventure" type of journey.

The tools and guides will be provided, but it is up to the church's Expedition Team to decide which tools are needed, which tools just need sharpening, which tools can stay in their backpack to use at a later time, what pathways to explore, and what pathways to pass.

The Greatest Expedition provides a new lens and updated tools to help your Expedition Team explore and think about being the church in different ways. Will your Expedition Team need to clear the overgrown brush from a once known trail, but not recently traveled? Or will the Expedition Team need to cut a brand new trail with their new tools? Or perhaps, will the Team decide they need to move to a completely fresh terrain and begin breaking ground for something brand new in a foreign climate?

Registration is open and Expedition Teams are launching!

greatestexpedition.com

Other Books From Phil Maynard

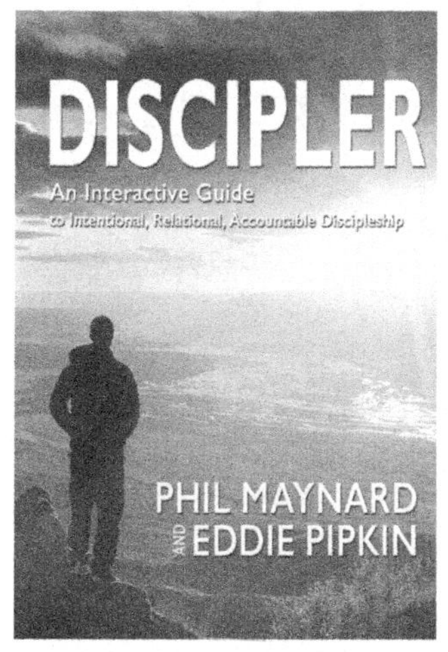

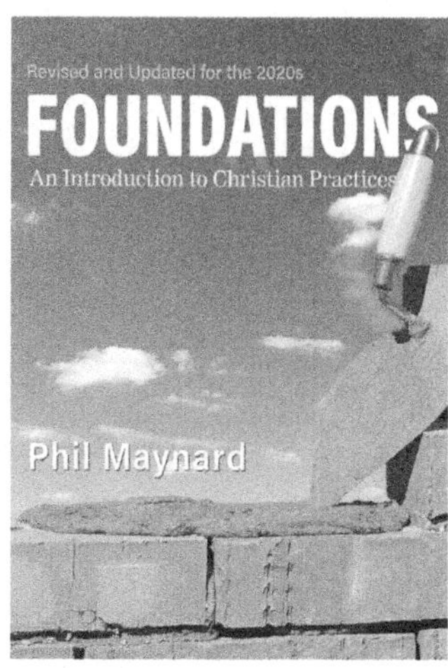

MarketSquareBooks.com

the greatest
EXPEDITION
A New Kind
of
Venture
Leader
Olu Brown

EXPANDING
THE
EXPEDITION
THROUGH
Digital
Ministry
Nicole Reilley
the greatest
EXPEDITION

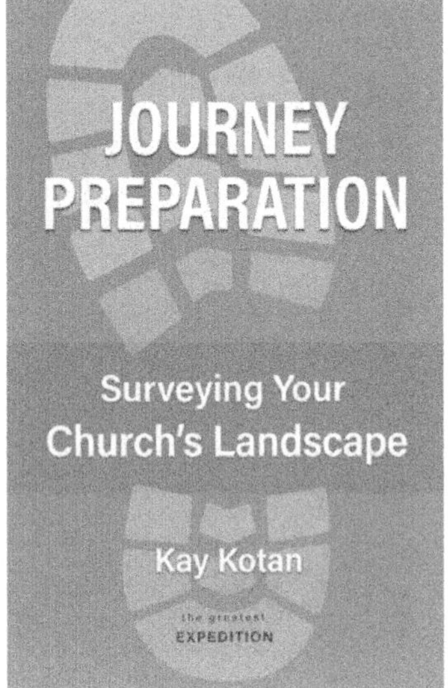
JOURNEY
PREPARATION
Surveying Your
Church's Landscape
Kay Kotan
the greatest
EXPEDITION

EQUIPPING
LAY
VENTURE
LEADERS
Kelly Brown
the greatest
EXPEDITION

Expanding
the Expedition
Reach
with Missional
Communities
Rachel Gilmore
the greatest
EXPEDITION

OPEN
ROAD
The Adventure of a
Breakthrough Prayer Initiative
Sue Nilson Kibbey

MULTI-SITE
MINISTRY
expanding the
Expedition Reach
KEN NASH
with Kristen Farrell
the greatest
EXPEDITION

CULTURAL
COMPETENCY
Partnering with your neighbors in your
Ministry Expedition
PAUL NIXON
the greatest
EXPEDITION

Made in the USA
Monee, IL
04 March 2022

92081453R00066